Forewo

Law Enforcement Response to Child Abuse —like all the Portable Guides in this series—is designed to assist those working to help protect children from being victimized and to improve the investigation of child abuse cases.

This guide arms law enforcement professionals with the information needed to ensure consistency in their investigation of child abuse. Pertinent considerations and helpful investigatory protocols are provided. Other useful materials include suggestions on working with physicians, responding to domestic disturbance calls, and placing children in protective custody. Supplemental readings and additional resources are cited.

In protecting our children from criminal predators, law enforcement professionals are serving their communities and their Nation. We hope that this guide will aid in that worthy endeavor.

Original Printing May 1997

Second Printing March 2001

NCJ 162425

C hild abuse is a *community* problem. No single agency has the training, manpower, resources, or legal mandate to intervene effectively in child abuse cases. No one agency has the sole responsibility for dealing with abused children.

When a child is physically beaten or sexually abused, the ideal set of events is that doctors treat the injuries, therapists counsel the child, social services works with the family, police arrest the offender, and attorneys prosecute the case. To promote this response, effective community intervention involves the formation of a child protection team that includes professionals from medicine, criminal justice, social work, and education who understand and appreciate the different roles, responsibilities, strengths, and weaknesses of the other team members but cooperate and coordinate their efforts. The skills of each person are viewed as different but equally important.

The role of law enforcement in child abuse cases is to investigate to determine if a violation of criminal law occurred, identify and apprehend the offender, and file appropriate criminal charges. The response of law enforcement to child abuse needs to be consistent. The intent of this guide is to provide officers who respond to this type of crime with information that will ensure this consistency. It is also to help law enforcement understand the importance of developing procedures and protocols and ways they can work with other professions to ensure that the needs of children are met.

Overview

1

State-mandated reporting laws require a referral when there is a suspicion of abuse. In most child abuse cases, law enforcement becomes involved in one of two ways: by a referral from a school, a physician, or an agency such as social services, or by a direct call for service from a parent, a child, or a neighbor. Because of increased reporting of child abuse, it is critical that police officers be trained to handle cases involving child maltreatment.

Child abuse cases have unique characteristics that make them different from other types of cases. For a number of reasons, children make "perfect" victims, and crimes involving child abuse, particularly sexual abuse, are among the most difficult investigated by law enforcement:

* Children are usually unable to protect themselves because of their level of physical and mental development; frequently they do not like to talk about the abuse. They may delay disclosure or tell only part of the story.

* An emotional bond often exists between the child and the offender; children may want the abuse to stop, but they may not want the offender to be punished.

* Crimes of abuse are not usually isolated incidents; instead, they take place over a period of time, often with increasing severity.

* In most sexual abuse cases, there is no conclusive medical evidence that sexual abuse occurred. Moreover, it occurs in a private place with no witnesses to the event.

* Interviews of children require special handling; legal issues governing child testimony are complicated and ever changing, and children—whether victims or witnesses—are often viewed as less credible or competent than the accused.

* Child abuse cases often involve concurrent civil, criminal, and sometimes administrative investigations; they often cross jurisdictional lines.

* The criminal justice system was not designed to handle the special needs of children.

Officers must be objective and proactive in their investigations of abuse. Questions concerning who, what, where, when, how, and why must be answered. It is important to remember that child abuse is a crime and law enforcement has a legal duty and responsibility to respond accordingly.

Multidisciplinary Team Approach

The most effective approach to cases involving child maltreatment is interagency coordination and planning. Social workers, physicians, therapists, prosecutors, judges, and police officers all have important roles to play. All must work together with a common concern—the welfare of the child—and with a common goal—to communicate with mutual respect. Differences of opinion are to be expected. Effective teamwork includes having a mechanism for discussing and, if possible, resolving these differences.

All members of the child protection team have an obligation to appreciate what the other professionals on the team are seeking to accomplish and to understand how their activities interrelate. For example, law enforcement officers need to be concerned that their investigation might traumatize a child, and physicians and therapists need to be concerned that their treatment and evaluation techniques might hinder or damage law enforcement's investigation. An ongoing discussion of problems that the team encounters during investigations will help resolve them and will also clarify the roles and responsibilities of team members.

All players on the child protection team must have clearly defined roles in order to carry out their responsibilities effectively.

* An interagency protocol helps in establishing written guidelines for those who investigate cases of child abuse and neglect.
* A properly drafted agreement also provides a blueprint for each of the principal agencies responsible for abuse cases in the community.

The team members must also invest their time in developing a long-range strategic plan that will ensure the team is ever responsive to the needs and changes within the community.

The goal should be efficient coordination of services, with the chief objectives being to determine what happened and to meet the needs of the child.

The following are essential elements of an effective interdisciplinary response team:

* Identification of the scope of the community problem.

* Identification of the resources available.

* Establishment of communication guidelines for each response team member and the victim's family.

* Establishment of clearly defined roles and responsibilities for each response team member.

* Establishment of clearly defined criteria for the types of cases with which the team will become involved.

Establishing Law Enforcement Protocols and Procedures

With their legal authority to investigate violations of the law, law enforcement officers are vital members of a community's child protection team. Failure to respond properly to child abuse cases from the outset (e.g., failure of the responding law enforcement officer to obtain certain information) can result in cases being dismissed in court or, in some cases, in innocent people being falsely accused.

Investigators should be trained and experienced in objectively investigating child maltreatment, including conducting interviews of children and interrogating suspected offenders. Training should be viewed as an ongoing process, designed to increase the competence of the interdisciplinary team.

Moreover, local law enforcement departments must establish policies and procedures to investigate child abuse cases. Personnel investigating child abuse need to consider many important factors (see figure 1, "Considerations for Child Abuse Investigations," pages 6 and 7).

Established agency protocols, guidelines, and training will guide the decisionmaking process, but officers are likely to face situations in which the officer's judgment must be the guiding light. For this reason, officers must be familiar with what is expected of them legally in their jurisdiction. As necessary, they should consult the agency's legal advisor or the prosecuting attorney to clarify this.

Speaking a Common Language

Professional terminology is used by many disciplines. Members of the child protection team must be familiar with highly specialized technical terms (such as "subdural hematoma," "dissociation," "battered child syndrome," and "pedophilia") as well as with basic or common terms (such as "child," "molestation," and "rape"). However, problems can arise because some terms do not have a universally accepted, consistent definition. It is important for clear communication and effective coordination that professional team members understand what is meant when professional terminology (or jargon) is used by other team members and that they ask for clarification when they do not.

The legal definition of a child varies from State to State and even from statute to statute in the same State. Issues such as whether the victim consented or whether the offender was a guardian or caretaker are important legal considerations in such cases. How the law determines consent is often confusing, even in the case of a 14-year-old boy who has been seduced by a 55-year-old pedophile. There is a difference between the legal definition of consent and the meaning given to it by lay people.

To determine who is a child and what is abuse, law enforcement officers must turn to the law. The penal code will legally define both, but law enforcement officers must still deal with their own perceptions and opinions as well as with those of society as a whole.

For this reason, people working as part of an interdisciplinary task force must clearly communicate how they are defining a particular term and establish common ground. Law enforcement investigators should always be aware of and communicate to others the legal definitions of terms.

Law enforcement investigators must also be able to communicate with victims, offenders, and witnesses, as well as with social workers, physicians, mental health personnel, lawyers, judges, and peers. To avoid confusion and misunderstanding, investigators must be equally familiar with various family or slang terms for body parts and sexual acts when talking to victims, witnesses, and suspects. Investigators must know not only both the slang and professional terms, but also the appropriate times for using each.

Considerations for Child Abuse Investigations

When You Receive the Referral

* Identify personal or professional biases with child abuse cases. Develop the ability to desensitize yourself to those issues and maintain an objective stance.

* Know department guidelines and State statutes.

* Know what resources are available in the community (therapy, victim compensation, etc.) and provide this information to the child's family.

* Introduce yourself, your role, and the focus and objective of the investigation.

* Assure that the best treatment will be provided for the protection of the child.

* Interview the child alone, focusing on corroborative evidence.

* Don't rule out the possibility of child abuse with a domestic dispute complaint; talk with the children at the scene.

Getting Information for the Preliminary Report

* Inquire about the history of the abusive situation. Dates are important to set the timeline for when abuse may have occurred.

* Cover the elements of crime necessary for the report. Inquire about the instrument of abuse or other items on the scene.

* Don't discount children's statements about who is abusing them, where and how the abuse is occurring, or what types of acts occurred.

* Save opinions for the end of the report, and provide supportive facts. Highlight the atmosphere of disclosure and the mood and demeanor of participants in the complaint.

Preserving the Crime Scene

* Treat the scene as a crime scene (even if abuse has occurred in the past) and not as the site of a social problem.

Figure 1 *continued*

* Secure the instrument of abuse or other corroborative evidence that the child identifies at the scene.

* Photograph the scene and, when appropriate, include any injuries to the child. Rephotograph injuries as needed to capture any changes in appearance.

Followup Investigation

* Be supportive and optimistic to the child and the family.

* Arrange for a medical examination and transportation to the hospital. Collect items for a change of clothes if needed.

* Make use of appropriate investigative techniques.

* Be sure the child and family have been linked to support services or therapy.

* Be sure the family know how to reach a detective to disclose further information.

During the Court Phase

* Visit the court with the child to familiarize him or her with the courtroom setting and atmosphere before the first hearing. This role may be assumed by the prosecutor or, in some jurisdictions, by victim/witness services.

* Prepare courtroom exhibits (pictures, displays, sketches) to support the child's testimony.

* File all evidence in accordance with State and court policy.

* Unless they are suspects, update the family about the status and progress of the investigation and stay in touch with them throughout the court process. Depending on the case, officers should be cautious about the type and amount of information provided to the family, since they may share the information with others.

* Provide court results and case closure information to the child and the family.

* Follow up with the probation department for preparation of the presentence report and victim impact statement(s).

Working With the Medical Profession

Physicians can be important allies in the prevention and treatment of child abuse. Doctors can serve as family counselors and educators, as influential child advocates, and as key members of the community multidisciplinary team. They can help to alleviate stress on a family by managing health problems, providing child-rearing advice, and discussing family planning alternatives.

In cases of suspected child maltreatment, doctors have five basic responsibilities:

* To identify suspicious injuries.

* To diagnose problems of abuse.

* To administer treatment to the child.

* To report suspected incidents of abuse to the appropriate authorities.

* To testify in subsequent legal proceedings.

Unfortunately, some physicians are reluctant to get involved in cases of abuse. For example, they may find few personal or professional rewards in dealing with an abusive family. They may not wish to report an incident because it may be impossible to determine who caused a child's injuries. Finally, they may not wish to testify in court because of time constraints or because of a fear of cross-examination, interrogation, challenges to their credentials, or possible litigation.

Law enforcement investigators can help counteract physicians' reluctance by fully involving members of the medical profession in the community's team approach to child abuse and by stressing the importance of medical evidence in preparing a case for court. It may also be helpful to remind physicians that all 50 States and the District of Columbia have enacted legislation regarding immunity from civil or criminal liability for persons who, in good faith, make or participate in making a report of child abuse or neglect.

Obtaining a Medical Examination

In most cases a medical assessment of the child needs to be performed as soon as possible. The primary purposes of the medical examination are to assess potential injury and identify the need for treatment. Such an examination will also protect law enforcement against accusations that a child's injuries occurred after removal from the home. Whenever possible, all children suspected of having been abused should be given a medical examination, preferably by a medical professional experienced and trained in conducting forensic examinations. This is critical in cases in which sexual abuse is alleged. The medical professional should reassure the child, who may be fearful about the procedure and concerned about the physical and emotional consequences of the abuse.

A secondary purpose of a medical examination is to determine the presence of any corroborating evidence of acute or chronic trauma. In recent years the ability and willingness of doctors to corroborate child abuse has improved greatly. Better training, the establishment of protocols, and technological advancements have improved the ability of doctors to corroborate physical and sexual abuse in children. Medical imaging technology now available includes magnetic resonance imaging (MRI), computed tomography (CT), and colposcopes (an instrument with magnification capabilities for visualizing the interior of a hollow organ, such as the vagina or rectum; pictures and video can be taken with the colposcope to document the examination results).

Law enforcement should be aware that statements made to doctors by the child during the medical examination may be admissible in court as exceptions to the hearsay rule. Many acts of child sexual abuse do not leave any physical injury that can be identified by a medical examination. In addition, children's injuries can heal rapidly. However, lack of medical corroboration does not necessarily mean that a child was not sexually abused or that an offense cannot be proved in court.

Figure 2, "Sample Child Sexual Abuse Protocol" (see pages 10 and 11), offers guidelines for the immediate law enforcement response to an allegation of child sexual abuse and provides details about obtaining the medical examination critical to investigating this offense.

Figure 2

Investigator's Sample
Child Sexual Assault Protocol

Interviewing the Victim

* Assess the medical needs of the child so that emergency medical conditions can be attended to immediately.
* Determine what examinations are needed for collection of evidence.
* Determine venue.
* Establish what offenses, if any, have occurred.
* Establish date and time of the offense.
* Contact child protective services (CPS), if that has not been done.

Obtaining a Medical Examination

Note: If a sexual assault occurred within the previous 72 hours, the medical examination should be performed as soon as possible to maximize the possibility of recovering certain forensic evidence, such as blood, semen, saliva, and trace evidence. If the assault occurred more than 72 hours before, the probability of this type of evidence being recovered is reduced. However, since the investigator cannot be absolutely sure when the last encounter was, it is prudent to schedule the medical examination sooner rather than later. A physician and/or nurse examiner conducts the examination.

* Contact a physician and/or sexual assault nurse examiner.
* Coordinate with CPS to determine if you (the police investigator) or the CPS worker will accompany the child to the examination.
* Meet with the CPS representative, the physician and/or nurse examiner, the child, and the parent or guardian at the hospital treatment room.
* Assist the child and parents or guardian with the procedures for admission to the emergency room. (CPS may provide this assistance, depending on who has requested the examination.)
* Brief medical personnel concerning the facts, allegations, suspect information, the mental state of the child, past histories, and what the police department and CPS are looking for in the examination and what evidence is to be collected.

Figure 2 *continued*

Handling the Evidence

✳ See that the cultures are prepared and marked to maintain the chain of custody. Include the date, the initials of the person conducting the examination, and the child's name. Transport the cultures and all other materials collected for evidence to the State laboratory. Make sure that both you and the laboratory personnel have signed the chain of custody form. Local procedures may differ from this; law enforcement must know and follow all jurisdictional procedures for handling evidence.

✳ Make sure that photographs are marked with the date, time, victim's name, photographer's initials, and case number and turned over to you as evidence. Photographs can be taken by police officers, investigators, CPS workers, physicians, nurse examiners, or other parties.

Subpoena Procedures

✳ Call the physician and/or nurse examiner as soon as possible if a subpoena has been issued to compare calendars and identify any conflicts early. Such notification should include the names of the child victim, defendant, and prosecuting attorney (if known); court date; and matters to which the physician may be requested to testify. Local procedures may differ from this; law enforcement must know and follow all practices and procedures for their jurisdiction.

✳ As an option, law enforcement may assist in the coordination of a pretrial conference with the medical professional and the prosecutor in advance of the court hearing. At this meeting:

- Questions that may be asked of the medical professional can be outlined.
- Medical terminology or difficult trial issues related to the testimony can be clarified.
- Requests for exhibits that may be helpful in clarifying testimony can be discussed and time allowed for their preparation.

This meeting is also a courtesy to prepare the medical professional in a timely fashion and to relieve the anxiety of testifying.

Domestic Disturbance Calls

One of the most common calls for service by law enforcement is the domestic disturbance call. Most police officers understand the potential for danger associated with such calls, but many do not realize that a violent adult might also vent anger on a child. A recent study in Florida* revealed that nearly one-third of domestic disturbance calls masked an incident of some form of child victimization. For this reason, officers should ask whether there are children living at the residence and, if so, where they are.

* It is recommended that domestic disturbance calls be answered with at least two officers, not only for officer protection but also so that one officer can deal with the parties involved with the domestic disturbance while the other officer talks with any children who may be present.

* Once the involved parties are calm, most parents, if asked tactfully, will allow an officer to talk with their children and may even appreciate the officer's offer to allay a child's fear that someone has been hurt or is going to jail.

* If possible, an officer should speak directly with the children. Such conversations allow the police officer to gather information about the situation directly from the child and to assess the child's need for protection.

Officers should be observant and look for any physical signs that the child may have been abused, but they should be aware that a child in this situation is likely to be afraid and withdrawn. Nervousness or a reluctance to talk to an officer does not mean that physical abuse has taken place. The officer should be attuned to the fact that the child may not want to stay at the residence, fearing another altercation.

An officer suspecting child abuse should preserve possible crime scene evidence such as a weapon or instrument of abuse and arrange for photographing of the scene. This eliminates the need for a search warrant, since officers are already legally on the scene. The officer must also notify social services of his or her suspicions of child abuse as soon as possible.

---

* Hammond CB, Poindexter RW, Caimano JV, Kramer LH, Turman KM, Wilson JJ, Bieck W, Hillsborough County Sheriff's Office, Tampa, Florida. *Crimes Against Children Crime Analysis Project: Implications and Findings.* Washington, DC: Office of Juvenile Justice and Delinquency Prevention, 1993.

Placing a Child in Emergency Protective Custody

Officers who become involved in a child abuse case through social services should consider all information that has been provided to them. Based on this information, officers should ask a basic question: "If we leave and obtain a court order to remove this child, is the child likely to be injured before we return?" If the answer is yes, then the officer should remove the child. All actions should be in accordance with State guidelines and departmental policy and procedure:

* Depending on the jurisdiction, the officer may be obligated to remove the child if direct disclosure of physical or sexual abuse is made, if such abuse is alleged, or if evidence of an abusive incident is present.

* Moreover, in most jurisdictions, State law allows an officer to decide to remove a child based on observation of the facts and judgment of the information given. In some situations an officer may remove a child because he or she feels that the child may suffer further physical or emotional harm or trauma or be hidden or abducted before a court order can be obtained.

In some jurisdictions law enforcement may be called upon by child protective services to investigate allegations of child abuse, to officially place a child in emergency protective custody, or to assist with such placement. Officers in such situations need to know the laws in their State. Failure to understand their legally mandated roles and responsibilities could result in:

* A child being left in a dangerous situation.

* A child being removed illegally.

* The officer and the department being placed in a situation of civil liability.

However, if a mistake is to be made, it is better to err in the attempt to safeguard the physical well-being of the child.

In jurisdictions where law enforcement has sole responsibility for deciding to remove a child from the home, the child is usually placed in the custody of the department of social services until a final determination regarding custody of the child can be made by the courts. Social services is responsible for placing the child in a licensed foster care facility. Officers need to be aware of the legalities regarding parental rights and their responsibilities for providing written notification of the child's removal.

In most States it is not acceptable for law enforcement to take a child from one parent and place him or her in the custody of another parent or of a relative without a court order or verification of legal authority. Also, in most States the placement of a child in the custody of another individual is the sole responsibility of the department of social services and not law enforcement. However, if social services chooses to place the child in the custody of a parent or someone other than a licensed foster care facility, law enforcement should be aware of the jurisdiction's policies and practices before participating in or agreeing to this placement.

It is highly recommended that removal or detention orders or other appropriate court paperwork accompany officers to the removal site and that this paperwork be explained to adversarial parents. In some jurisdictions there is "summary removal" authority—that is, with no paperwork in hand and based on circumstances of the case as it develops, the child may be removed from the home. Safety issues enter into the equation, especially as law enforcement is often present for the protection of social service personnel.

Law enforcement officers are responsible for ensuring that they have met all requirements of their State governing the placement of children into protective custody.

Common Mistakes To Avoid

Some law enforcement officers inadvertently cause a situation to escalate when placing a child in protective custody. Experienced officers have learned to avoid three common mistakes:

❋ **Making premature accusations.** Making an accusatory statement to the parent, guardian, or custodian that the child is being taken into protective custody because someone has abused the child places police officers in a situation of serious liability. A more appropriate statement is, "Because of questionable injuries, marks, or allegations about inappropriate activity, the child is being taken to a licensed foster care facility of the State until a complete and thorough investigation into the situation can be conducted."

* **Attempting to rationalize the removal of a child.** Some officers attempt to rationalize with the parent their decision to remove a child. However, the best tactic is to remove the child and vacate the situation as quickly as possible, after ensuring that everyone's rights are protected. The fact is that no amount of explaining will lessen the pain, fear, and anger (hostility) involved in having a child taken away. Officers should be aware that heightened emotions can lead to a dangerous escalation of the situation.

* **Failing to provide all of the required forms.** Police officers must be familiar with all the forms that must be completed by the parent at the time that a child is placed in protective custody. For example, many States require that a form explaining that the child has been placed in protective custody must be provided to the parents within 24 hours after the child has been so placed. The form must state that the placement was made in accordance with a particular statute, and it must describe the parents' rights in the matter. The responsibility for providing this form to the parents varies from State to State. Law enforcement officers and social service workers must know what is required in their State.

Removing the Child

If a law enforcement officer has been called to assist in the removal of a child, it is the officer's responsibility to ensure that the child is removed with as little trauma or danger to the child and the social worker as possible.

* The police officer should meet with the social worker at a neutral location before going to the residence. The social worker should explain the situation in general, describe the layout of the residence, and specify who is expected to be there. In this way the police officer and the social worker can determine a plan of action before arriving at the scene.

* Any necessary items, such as medication, should be brought with the child. The key point is that once the decision to remove a child has been made, the action should be carried out expeditiously.

Impact on the Child

Physical removal from the home is extremely traumatic for the child. Both the law enforcement officer and the social worker are relative strangers. They need to keep the following points in mind:

* Debating the situation with the parent or caretaker only raises the emotional level of the child. Such arguments may cause the child to become more nervous, upset, distraught, and emotionally unstable.

* In most situations, children are not going to leave their parents willingly, even though they have been physically or sexually abused. They may not understand what is best for them and may try to resist the law enforcement officer.

* Officers should not respond to a child's outbursts with anger or displeasure. Instead, they should behave as positively—or at least neutrally—as possible. They should do everything they can to help the child adjust to a new and scary situation.

* Once the officer has removed the child from the residence and the child has had a chance to calm down, if the child is old enough to communicate, the officer should take the time to explain that the child has not done anything wrong and was removed for his or her own protection.

Conclusion

Child abuse is a multidimensional problem that requires a multidisciplinary, multiagency team approach for successful intervention. This means that all professionals involved — in law enforcement, child protective services, mental health, medicine, and the law—communicate and coordinate with one another. A child's best interest can be served only when the various professionals that are involved understand their respective roles, possess knowledge of their State statutes and local guidelines, and have adequate training in their respective fields. Sensitive and consistent application of policies and procedures established in written protocols is essential for an effective alliance to combat child maltreatment.

Contributing Authors

Carl B. Hammond
Law Enforcement Consultant/Trainer
P.O. Box 5332
Rockville, MD 20848–5332
301–468–3416

Kenneth V. Lanning, M.S. (Retired)

Wayne Promisel, M.S.
Detective, Child Services Section
Fairfax County Police Department
10600 Page Avenue
Fairfax, VA 22030
703–246–7813

Jack R. Shepherd
Captain
Executive Division
Michigan State Police
714 South Harrison Road
East Lansing, MI 48823
517–336–6552

Bill Walsh
Lieutenant, Dallas Police Department
Youth and Family Crimes Division
106 South Harwood Street, Room 225
Dallas, TX 75201
214–670–5391

Supplemental Reading

Besharov DJ. *Combating Child Abuse: Guidelines for Cooperation Between Law Enforcement and Child Protective Agencies.* Washington, DC: AEI Press, 1990.

Briere J, Berliner L, Bulkley J, Jenny C, Reid T (eds). *APSAC Handbook on Child Maltreatment.* Newbury Park, CA: Sage Publications, 1996.

Bryan J. *Team Investigation in Child Sexual Abuse Cases: A Desk Reference for Law Enforcement Officers, Protective Service Workers, and Prosecuting Attorneys.* Little Rock, AR: Arkansas Child Sexual Abuse Commission, 1987.

Center for the Future of Children. *Sexual Abuse of Children.* Newbury Park, CA: Center for the Future of Children, the David and Lucille Packard Foundation, 1994.

Child Abuse and Neglect State Statute Series. A joint project of the National Center on Child Abuse and Neglect (NCCAN) and the National Center for Prosecution of Child Abuse (NCPCA), this five-volume series summarizes State statutes on child abuse and neglect in nontechnical language: Volume I, Reporting Laws; Volume II, Central Registries; Volume III, Investigations; Volume IV, Child Witnesses; Volume V, Crimes. The series is updated annually and is available from the National Clearinghouse on Child Abuse and Neglect Information, 800–FYI–3366.

DePanfilis D, Salus MK. *A Coordinated Response to Child Abuse and Neglect: A Basic Manual* (The User Manual Series). Washington, DC: U.S. Department of Health and Human Services, Administration on Children, Youth and Families, National Center on Child Abuse and Neglect, 1992.

Myers JEB. *Legal Issues in Child Abuse and Neglect.* Newbury Park, CA: Sage Publications, 1992.

Pence D, Wilson C. *The Role of Law Enforcement in the Response to Child Abuse and Neglect.* (The User Manual Series). Washington, DC: U.S. Department of Health and Human Services, Administration for Children and Families, Administration on Children, Youth, and Families, National Center on Child Abuse and Neglect, 1992.

Pence D, Wilson C. *Team Investigation of Child Sexual Abuse.* Newbury Park, CA: Sage Publications, 1994.

Shepherd JR, Dworin B, Farley RH, Russ BJ, Tressler PW, National Center for Missing and Exploited Children. *Child Abuse and Exploitation: Investigative Techniques.* 2d ed. Washington, DC: Office of Juvenile Justice and Delinquency Prevention, 1995.

Smith JC, Benton RL, Moore JK, Runyan DK, American Association for Protecting Children. *Understanding the Medical Diagnosis of Child Maltreatment: A Guide for Non-Medical Professionals.* Englewood, CO: American Humane Association, 1989.

Whitcomb D. *When the Victim is a Child.* 2d ed. Washington, DC: U.S. Department of Justice, Office of Justice Programs, National Institute of Justice, 1992.

Wycoff MA, Kealoha M. *Creating the Multidisciplinary Response to Child Sex Abuse: An Implementation Guide.* Washington, DC: Police Foundation, 1987.

Organizations

National Center for the Prosecution of Child Abuse
American Prosecutors Research Institute (APRI)
99 Canal Center Plaza, Suite 510
Alexandria, VA 22314
703–549–4253
703–549–6259 (fax)

The National Center for the Prosecution of Child Abuse is a nonprofit and technical assistance affiliate of APRI. In addition to research and technical assistance, the Center provides extensive training on the investigation and prosecution of child abuse and child deaths. The national trainings include timely information presented by a variety of professionals experienced in the medical, legal, and investigative aspects of child abuse.

Federal Bureau of Investigation
935 Pennsylvania Avenue NW.
Washington, DC 20535–0001
202–324–3000

Forensic examination of evidence can be useful in cases of child sexual abuse. Tests that may be considered include:

* DNA profiling of body fluids or biological stains.

* Comparative examination of foreign hairs and fibers with those of a suspected source.

* Chemical analyses for petroleum jelly or lotion residues.

Questions on submission of these types of evidence can be directed to your local crime laboratory or to the FBI Laboratory at the number given above.

Fox Valley Technical College
Criminal Justice Department
Law Enforcement Training Programs
P.O. Box 2277
1825 North Bluemound Drive
Appleton, WI 54914–2277
800–648–4966
920–735–4757 (fax)

Participants are trained in child abuse and exploitation investigative techniques, covering the following areas:

* Recognition of signs of abuse.

* Collection and preservation of evidence.

* Preparation of cases for prosecution.

✳ Techniques for interviewing victims and offenders.

✳ Liability issues.

Fox Valley also offers an intensive special training for local child investigative teams. Teams must include representatives from law enforcement, prosecution, social services, and (optionally) the medical field. Participants take part in hands-on team activity involving:

✳ Development of interagency processes and protocols for enhanced enforcement, prevention, and intervention in child abuse cases.

✳ Case preparation and prosecution.

✳ Development of the team's own interagency implementation plan for improved investigation of child abuse.

National Children's Advocacy Center (NCAC)
Training Department
200 Westside Square, Suite 700
Huntsville, AL 35801
256–533–0531

NCAC sponsors satellite video training conferences on a range of topics. Recent examples include interviewing children, medical aspects of child abuse, team-building for multidisciplinary teams, and the connections between domestic violence and child sexual abuse. Continuing education credits are available.

Other Titles in This Series

Currently there are 12 other Portable Guides to Investigating Child Abuse. To obtain a copy of any of the guides listed below (in order of publication), contact the Office of Juvenile Justice and Delinquency Prevention's Juvenile Justice Clearinghouse by telephone at 800–638–8736 or e-mail at puborder@ncjrs.org.

Recognizing When a Child's Injury or Illness Is Caused by Abuse, NCJ 160938

Sexually Transmitted Diseases and Child Sexual Abuse, NCJ 160940

Photodocumentation in the Investigation of Child Abuse, NCJ 160939

Diagnostic Imaging of Child Abuse, NCJ 161235

Battered Child Syndrome: Investigating Physical Abuse and Homicide, NCJ 161406

Interviewing Child Witnesses and Victims of Sexual Abuse, NCJ 161623

Child Neglect and Munchausen Syndrome by Proxy, NCJ 161841

Criminal Investigation of Child Sexual Abuse, NCJ 162426

Burn Injuries in Child Abuse, NCJ 162424

Understanding and Investigating Child Sexual Exploitation, NCJ 162427

Forming a Multidisciplinary Team To Investigate Child Abuse, NCJ 170020

Use of Computers in the Sexual Exploitation of Children, NCJ 170021

Additional Resources

American Bar Association
(ABA)
Center on Children and
the Law
Washington, DC
202–662–1720
202–662–1755 (fax)

American Humane Association
Englewood, Colorado
800–227–4645
303–792–9900
303–792–5333 (fax)

American Medical Association
(AMA)
Department of Mental Health
Chicago, Illinois
312–464–5000
(AMA main number)
312–464–4184 (fax)

American Professional Society
on the Abuse of Children
(APSAC)
Oklahoma City, Oklahoma
405–271–8202
405–271–2931 (fax)

Federal Bureau of Investigation
(FBI)
National Center for the
Analysis of Violent Crime
Quantico, Virginia
703–632–4333

Fox Valley Technical College
Criminal Justice Department
Appleton, Wisconsin
800–648–4966
920–735–4757 (fax)

Juvenile Justice Clearinghouse
(JJC)
Rockville, Maryland
800–638–8736
301–519–5600 (fax)

Kempe Children's Center
Denver, Colorado
303–864–5252
303–864–5302 (fax)

National Association of Medical
Examiners
St. Louis, Missouri
314–577–8298
314–268–5124 (fax)

National Center for Missing
and Exploited Children
(NCMEC)
Alexandria, Virginia
703–274–3900
703–274–2220 (fax)

National Center for the
Prosecution of Child Abuse
Alexandria, Virginia
703–549–4253
703–549–6259 (fax)

National Children's Alliance
Washington, DC
800–239–9950
202–639–0597
202–639–0511 (fax)

National Clearinghouse on
Child Abuse and Neglect
Information
Washington, DC
800–FYI–3366
703–385–7565
703–385–3206 (fax)

National SIDS Resource
Center
Vienna, Virginia
703–821–8955, ext. 249
703–821–2098 (fax)

Prevent Child Abuse America
Chicago, Illinois
800–835–2671
312–663–3520
312–939–8962 (fax)

Made in the USA
Las Vegas, NV
31 March 2022